BACH: SELECTIONS FROM THE LUTE, VIOLIN, AND CELLO SUITES

for

EASY CLASSICAL GUITAR

CONTENTS

Editor's Note: For the sake of minimizing page turns,
"Bourrée II" from Cello Suite No. 4 has been placed out of sequence.

Arranged by Arthur Rotfeld
(Additional arranging by Mark Phillips)

Cherry Lane Music Company
Director of Publications/Project Editor: Mark Phillips

ISBN 978-1-60378-977-6

Visit our website at www.cherrylaneprint.com

Lute Suite No. 1, BWV 996 "Courante"

TRACK 1

Johann Sebastian Bach

Slowly, in 3

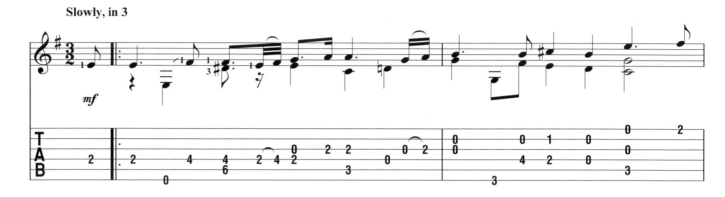

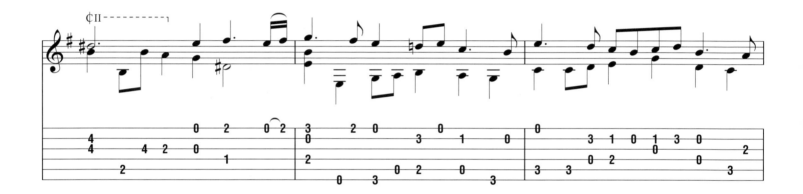

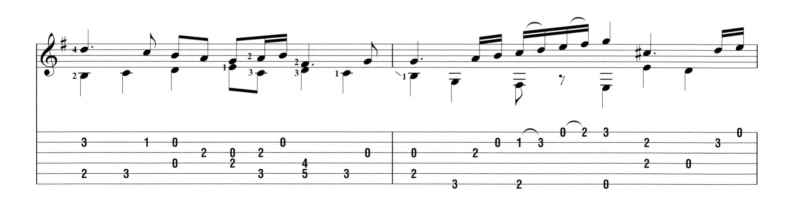

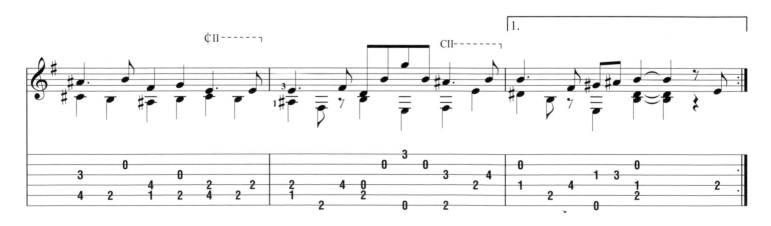

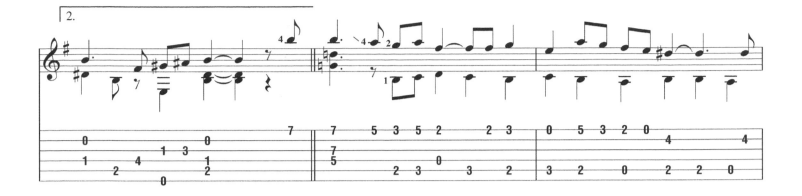

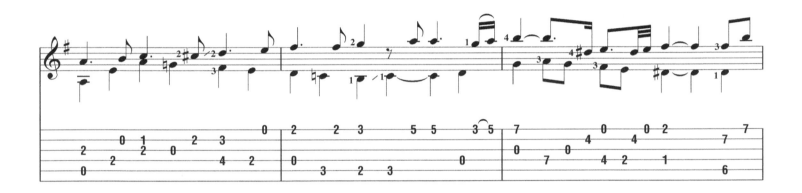

Lute Suite No. 1, BWV 996 "Sarabande"

Johann Sebastian Bach

TRACK 2

Slowly, in 3

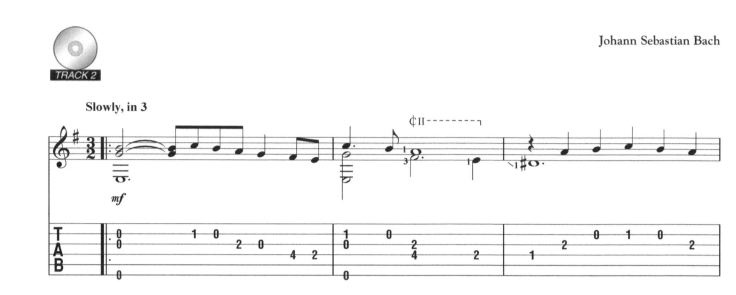

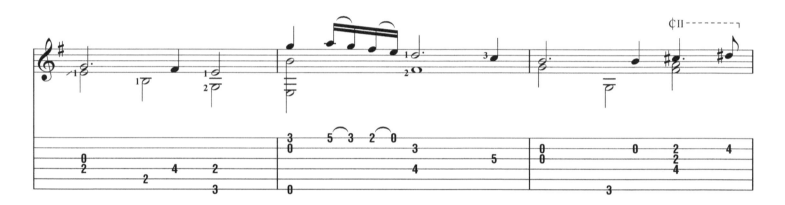

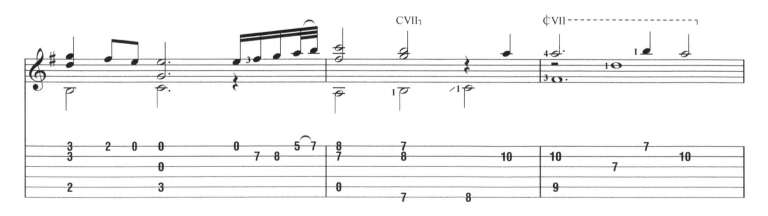

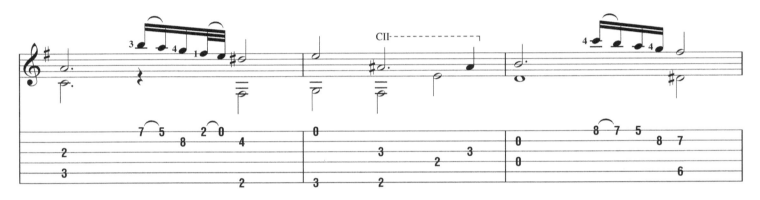

Lute Suite No. 1, BWV 996 "Bourrée"

Johann Sebastian Bach

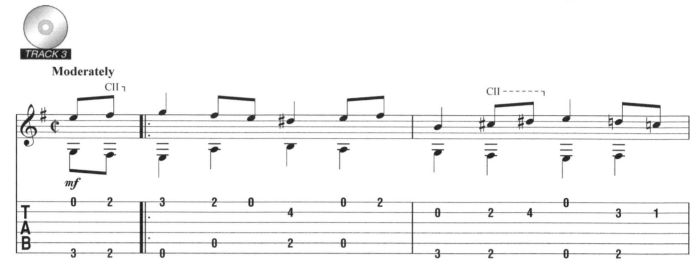

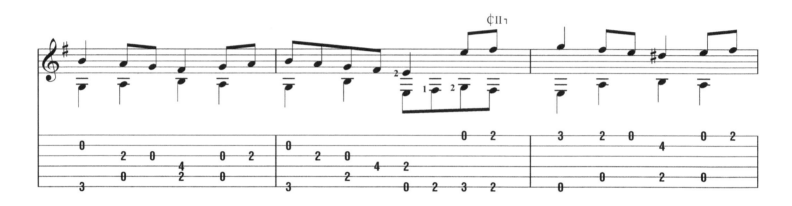

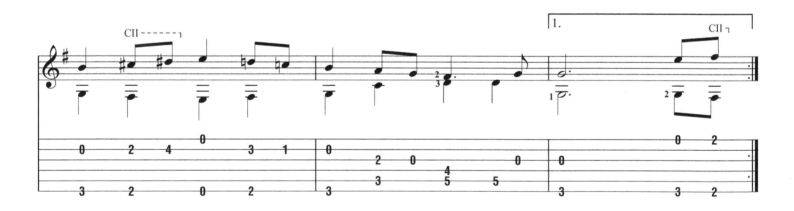

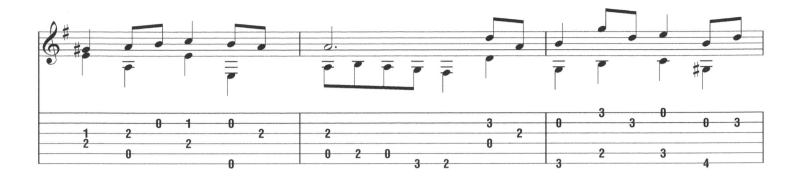

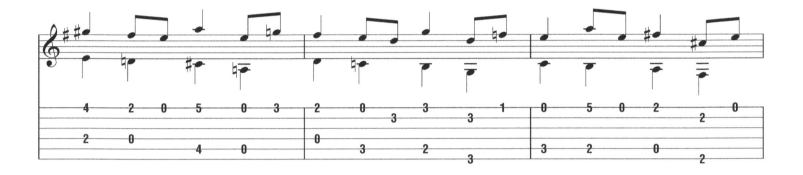

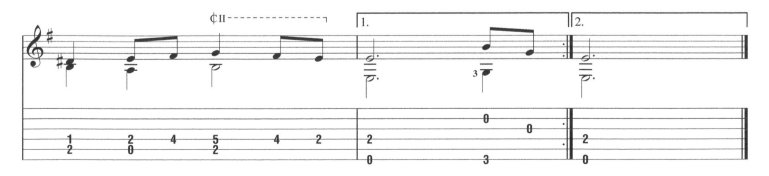

Lute Suite No. 2, BWV 997 "Gigue"

Johann Sebastian Bach

TRACK 4

Moderately, in 2

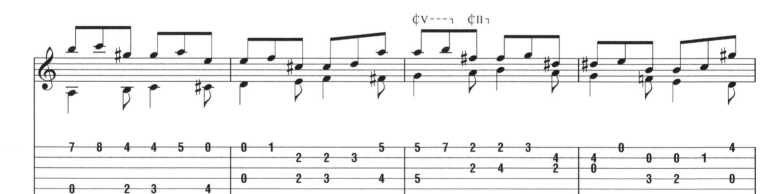

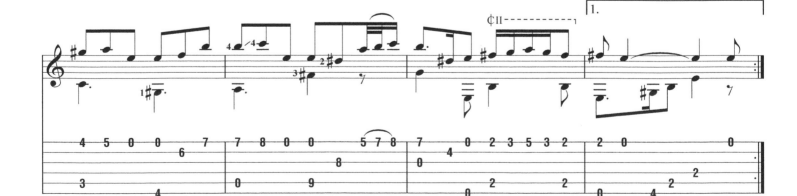

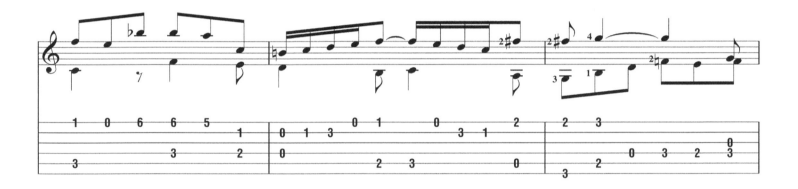

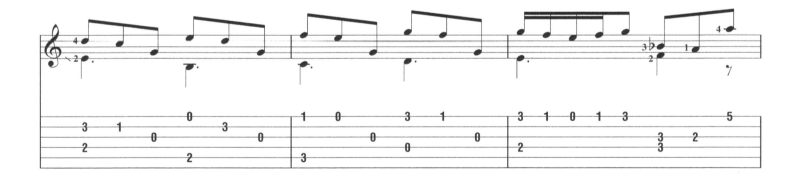

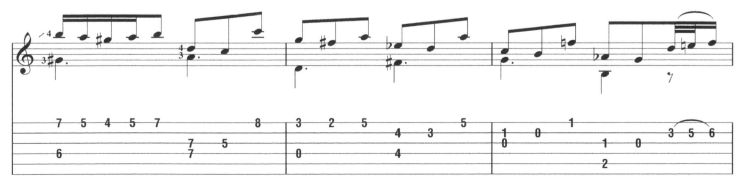

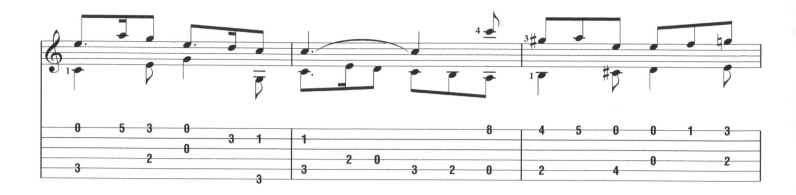

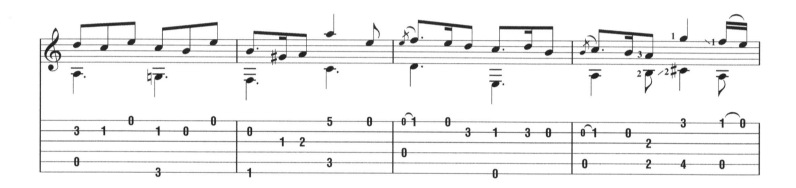

Cello Suite No. 4, BWV 1010 "Bourrée II"

Johann Sebastian Bach

Violin Partita No. 1, BWV 1002 "Sarabande"

Johann Sebastian Bach

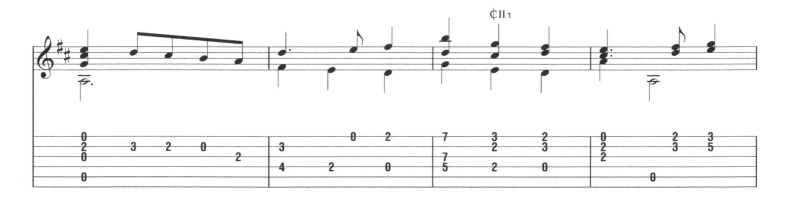

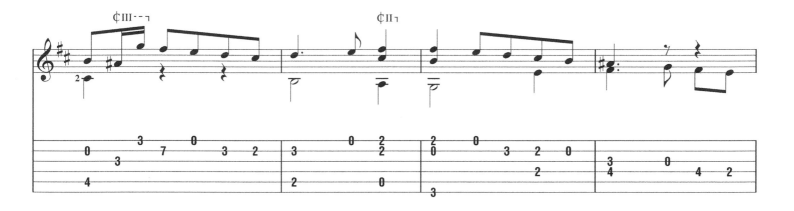

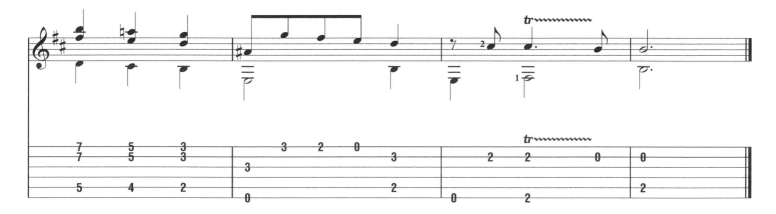

Violin Partita No. 1, BWV 1002
"Tempo di Bourrée"

Johann Sebastian Bach

Moderately bright

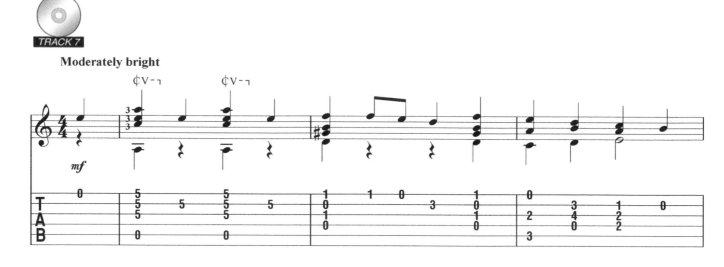

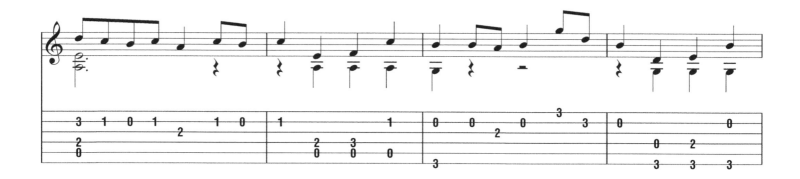

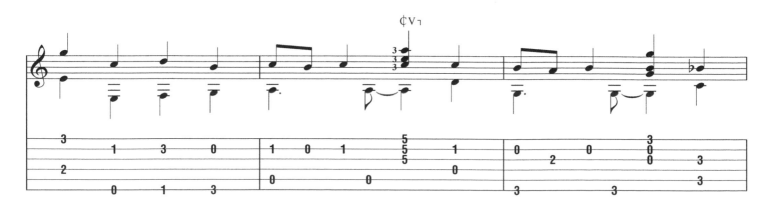

Violin Partita No. 2, BWV 1004 "Chaconne"

Johann Sebastian Bach

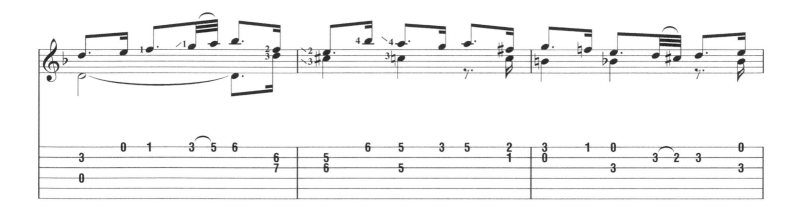

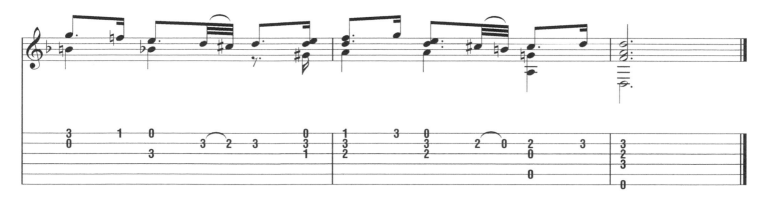

Cello Suite No. 2, BWV 1008 "Sarabande"

Johann Sebastian Bach

TRACK 9

Slowly

Cello Suite No. 2, BWV 1008 "Minuet I"

Johann Sebastian Bach

TRACK 10

Moderately slow

Cello Suite No. 3, BWV 1009 "Sarabande"

Johann Sebastian Bach

TRACK 11

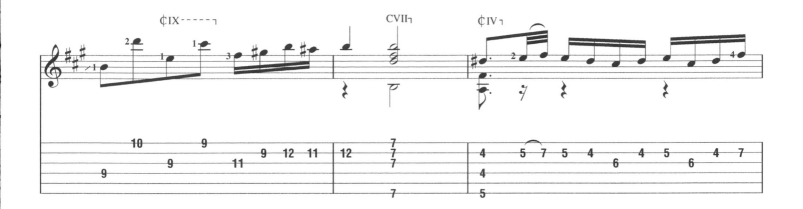

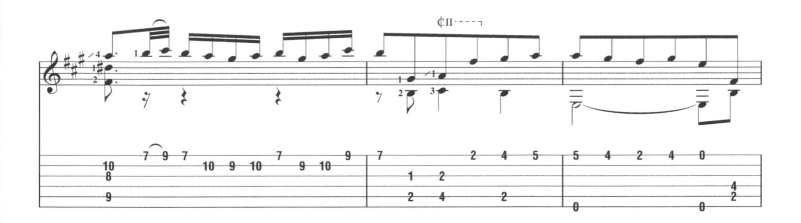

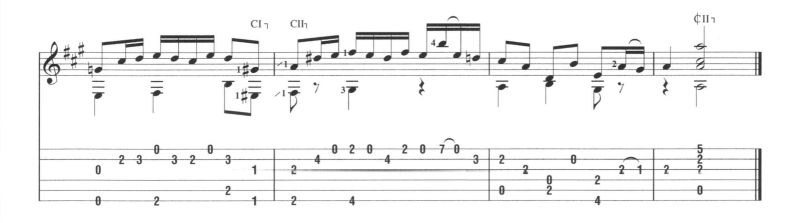

Cello Suite No. 3, BWV 1009 "Bourrée 1"

Johann Sebastian Bach

TRACK 12

Moderately

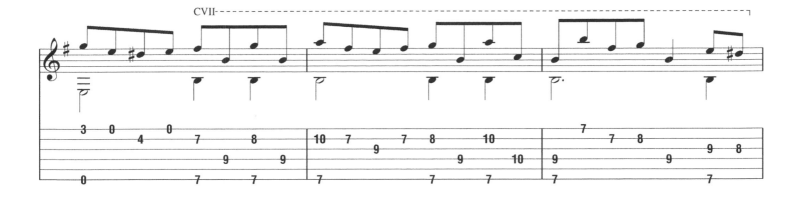

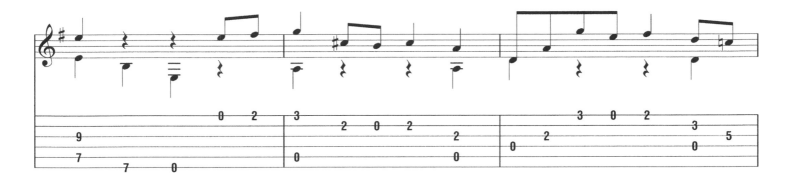

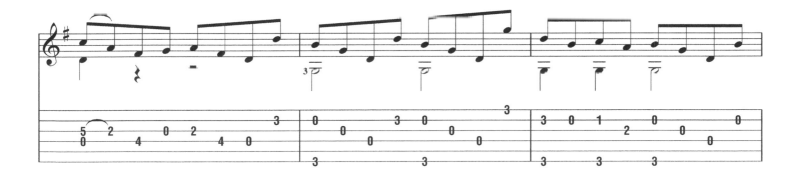

Cello Suite No. 5, BWV 1011 "Gavotte I"

Johann Sebastian Bach

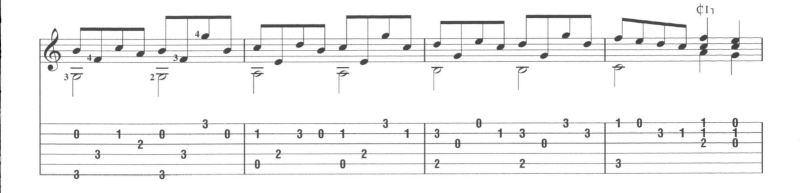

27

Cello Suite No. 6, BWV 1012 "Sarabande"

Johann Sebastian Bach

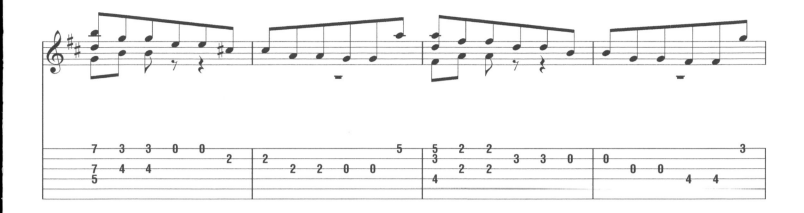

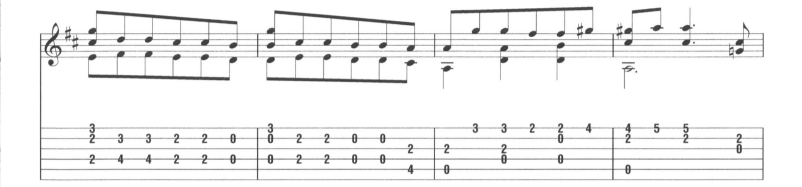

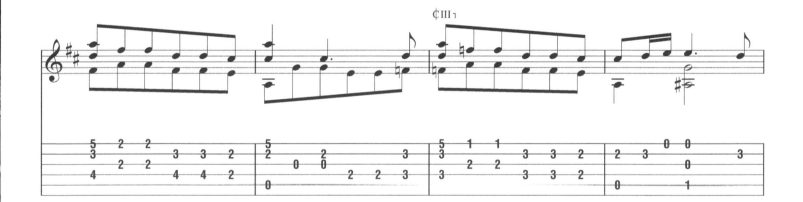

Cello Suite No. 6, BWV 1012 "Gavotte I"

Johann Sebastian Bach

TRACK 15

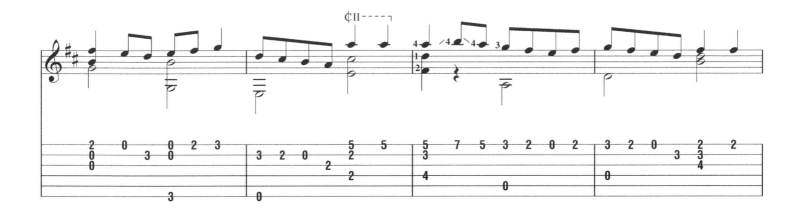

Cello Suite No. 6, BWV 1012 "Gavotte II"

Johann Sebastian Bach

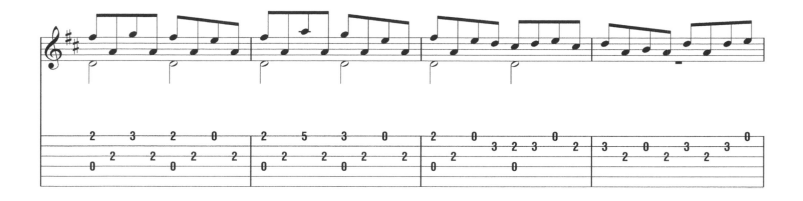

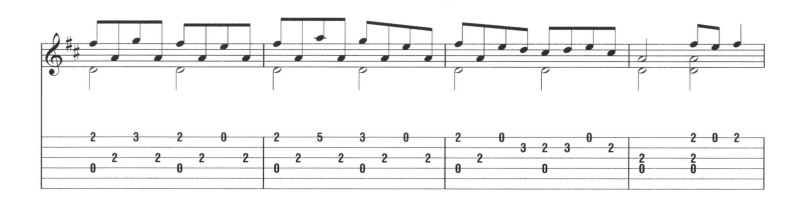

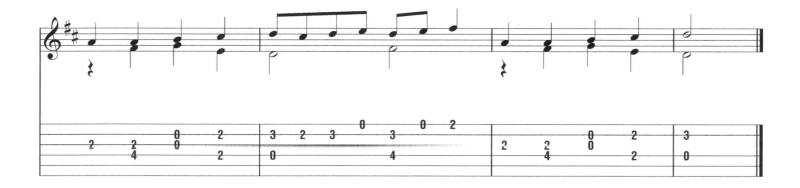

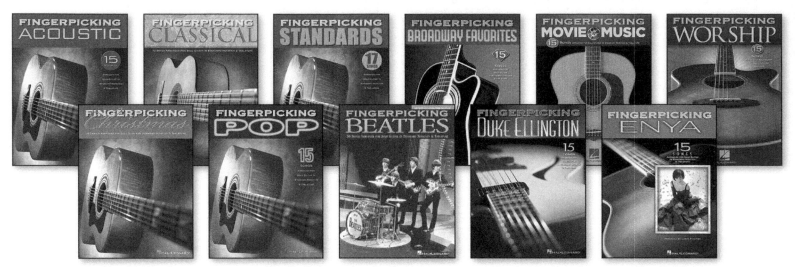

THE PUBLICATIONS OF
CHRISTOPHER PARKENING

CHRISTOPHER PARKENING – DUETS AND CONCERTOS

Throughout his career, Christopher Parkening has had the opportunity to perform with many of the world's leading artists and orchestras, and this folio contains many selections from those collaborations. All of the pieces included here have been edited and fingered for the guitar by Christopher Parkening himself.
00690938..$24.99

THE CHRISTOPHER PARKENING GUITAR METHOD, VOL. 1 – REVISED

in collaboration with
Jack Marshall and David Brandon

Learn the art of the classical guitar with this premier method for beginners by one of the world's preeminent virtuosos and the recognized heir to the legacy of Andrés Segovia. Learn basic classical guitar technique by playing beautiful pieces of music, including over 50 classical pieces, 26 exercises, and 14 duets. Includes notes in the first position, how to hold the guitar, tuning, right and left hand technique, arpeggios, tone production, placement of fingers and nails, flats, naturals, key signatures, the bar, and more. Also includes many helpful photos and illustrations, plus sections on the history of the classical guitar, selecting a guitar, guitar care, and more.
00695228..$12.95

THE CHRISTOPHER PARKENING GUITAR METHOD, VOL. 2

Intermediate to Upper-Intermediate Level

Continues where Vol. 1 leaves off. Teaches: all notes in the upper position; tone production; advanced techniques such as tremolo, harmonics, vibrato, pizzicato and slurs; practice tips; stylistic interpretation; and more. The first half of the book deals primarily with technique, while the second half of the book applies the technique with repertoire pieces. As a special bonus, this book includes 32 previously unpublished Parkening edition pieces by composers including Dowland, Bach, Scarlatti, Sor, Tarrega and other, plus three duets for two guitars.
00695229..$12.95

PARKENING AND THE GUITAR – VOL. 1

Music of Two Centuries:
Popular New Transcriptions for Guitar
Virtuoso Music for Guitar

Ten transcriptions for solo guitar of beautiful music from many periods and styles, edited and fingered by Christopher Parkening. All pieces are suitable for performance by the advanced guitarist. Ten selections: Afro-Cuban Lullaby • Empress of the Pagodes (Ravel) • Menuet (Ravel) • Minuet in D (Handel) • Passacaille (Weiss) • Pastourelle (Poulenc) • Pavane for a Dead Princess (Ravel) • Pavane for a Sleeping Beauty (Ravel) • Preambulo (Scarlatti-Ponce) • Sarabande (Handel).
00699105..$9.95

PARKENING AND THE GUITAR – VOL. 2

Music of Two Centuries: Popular New Transcriptions for Guitar
Virtuoso Music for Guitar

Nine more selections for the advanced guitarist: Clair de Lune (Debussy) • Giga (Visée) • The Girl with the Flaxen Hair (Debussy) • Gymnopedie Nos. I-III (Satie) • The Little Shepherd (Debussy) • The Mysterious Barricades (Couperin) • Sarabande (Debussy).
00699106..$9.95

CHRISTOPHER PARKENING – ROMANZA

Virtuoso Music for Guitar

Three wonderful transcriptions edited and fingered by Parkening: Catalonian Song • Rumores de la Caleta • Romance.
00699103..$7.95

CHRISTOPHER PARKENING – SACRED MUSIC FOR THE GUITAR, VOL. 1

Seven inspirational arrangements, transcriptions and compositions covering traditional Christian melodies from several centuries. These selections appear on the Parkening album Sacred Music for the Guitar. Includes: Präludium (Bach) • Our Great Savior • God of Grace and God of Glory (2 guitars) • Brethren, We Have Met to Worship • Deep River • Jesus, We Want to Meet • Evening Prayer.
00699095..$10.95

CHRISTOPHER PARKENING – SACRED MUSIC FOR THE GUITAR, VOL. 2

Seven more selections from the album *Sacred Music for the Guitar*: Hymn of Christian Joy (guitar and harpsichord) • Simple Gifts • Fairest Lord Jesus • Stir Thy Church, O God Our Father • All Creatures of Our God and King • Glorious Things of Thee Are Spoken • Praise Ye the Lord (2 guitars).
00699100..$10.95

CHRISTOPHER PARKENING – SOLO PIECES

Sixteen transcriptions for solo guitar edited and fingered by Parkening, including: Allegro • Danza • Fugue • Galliard • I Stand at the Threshold • Prelude • Sonata in D • Suite Española • Suite in D Minor • and more.
00690939..$19.95

PARKENING PLAYS BACH

Virtuoso Music for Guitar

Nine transcriptions edited and fingered by Parkening: Preludes I, VI & IX • Gavottes I & II • Jesu, Joy of Man's Desiring • Sheep May Safely Graze • Wachet Auf, Ruft Uns Die Stemme • Be Thou with Me • Sleepers Awake (2 guitars).
00699104..$9.95

CLASSICAL GUITAR

PUBLICATIONS FROM HAL LEONARD

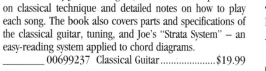

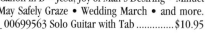
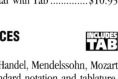
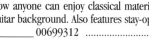

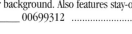
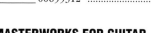

THE BEATLES FOR CLASSICAL GUITAR

Includes 20 solos from big Beatles hits arranged for classical guitar, complete with left-hand and right-hand fingering. Songs include: All My Loving • And I Love Her • Can't Buy Me Love • Fool on the Hill • From a Window • Hey Jude • If I Fell • Let It Be • Michelle • Norwegian Wood • Obla Di • Ticket to Ride • Yesterday • and more. Features arrangements and an introduction by Joe Washington, as well as his helpful hints on classical technique and detailed notes on how to play each song. The book also covers parts and specifications of the classical guitar, tuning, and Joe's "Strata System" – an easy-reading system applied to chord diagrams.

_____ 00699237 Classical Guitar $19.99

CZERNY FOR GUITAR

12 SCALE STUDIES FOR CLASSICAL GUITAR
by David Patterson

Adapted from Carl Czerny's *School of Velocity, Op. 299* for piano, this lesson book explores 12 keys with 12 different approaches or "treatments." You will explore a variety of articulations, ranges and technical perspectives as you learn each key. These arrangements will not only improve your ability to play scales fluently, but will also develop your ears, knowledge of the fingerboard, reading abilities, strength and endurance. In standard notation and tablature.

_____ 00701248 ....$9.99

MATTEO CARCASSI – 25 MELODIC AND PROGRESSIVE STUDIES, OP. 60

arr. Paul Henry

One of Carcassi's (1792-1853) most famous collections of classical guitar music – indispensable for the modern guitarist's musical and technical development. Performed by Paul Henry. 49-minute audio accompaniment.

_____ 00696506 Book/CD Pack $17.95

CLASSICAL & FINGERSTYLE GUITAR TECHNIQUES

by David Oakes • Musicians Institute

This Master Class with MI instructor David Oakes is aimed at any electric or acoustic guitarist who wants a quick, thorough grounding in the essentials of classical and fingerstyle technique. Topics covered include: arpeggios and scales, free stroke and rest stroke, P-i scale technique, three-to-a-string patterns, natural and artificial harmonics, tremolo and rasgueado, and more. The book includes 12 intensive lessons for right and left hand in standard notation & tab, and the CD features 92 solo acoustic tracks.

_____ 00695171 Book/CD Pack $17.99

CLASSICAL GUITAR CHRISTMAS COLLECTION

Includes classical guitar arrangements in standard notation and tablature for more than two dozen beloved carols: Angels We Have Heard on High • Auld Lang Syne • Ave Maria • Away in a Manger • Canon in D • The First Noel • God Rest Ye Merry, Gentlemen • Hark! the Herald Angels Sing • I Saw Three Ships • Jesu, Joy of Man's Desiring • Joy to the World • O Christmas Tree • O Holy Night • Silent Night • What Child Is This? • and more.

_____ 00699493 Guitar Solo $9.95

CLASSICAL GUITAR WEDDING

Perfect for players hired to perform for someone's big day, this songbook features 16 classsical wedding favorites arranged for solo guitar in standard notation and tablature. Includes: Air on the G String • Ave Maria • Bridal Chorus • Canon in D • Jesu, Joy of Man's Desiring • Minuet • Sheep May Safely Graze • Wedding March • and more.

_____ 00699563 Solo Guitar with Tab $10.95

CLASSICAL MASTERPIECES FOR GUITAR

27 works by Bach, Beethoven, Handel, Mendelssohn, Mozart and more transcribed with standard notation and tablature. Now anyone can enjoy classical material regardless of their guitar background. Also features stay-open binding.

_____ 00699312 ....$12.95

MASTERWORKS FOR GUITAR

Over 60 Favorites from Four Centuries
World's Great Classical Music

Dozens of classical masterpieces: Allemande • Bourree • Canon in D • Jesu, Joy of Man's Desiring • Lagrima • Malaguena • Mazurka • Piano Sonata No. 14 in C# Minor (Moonlight) Op. 27 No. 2 First Movement Theme • Ode to Joy • Prelude No. I (Well-Tempered Clavier).

_____ 00699503 ....$16.95

A MODERN APPROACH TO CLASSICAL GUITAR

by Charles Duncan

This multi-volume method was developed to allow students to study the art of classical guitar within a new, more contemporary framework. For private, class or self-instruction. Book One incorporates chord frames and symbols, as well as a recording to assist in tuning and to provide accompaniments for at-home practice. Book One also introduces beginning fingerboard technique and music theory. Book Two and Three build upon the techniques learned in Book One.

_____ 00695114 Book 1 – Book Only...............$6.99
_____ 00695113 Book 1 – Book/CD Pack $10.99
_____ 00695116 Book 2 – Book Only...............$6.99
_____ 00695115 Book 2 – Book/CD Pack $10.99
_____ 00699202 Book 3 – Book Only...............$7.95
_____ 00695117 Book 3 – Book/CD Pack $10.95
_____ 00695119 Composite Book/CD Pack.....$29.99

ANDRES SEGOVIA – 20 STUDIES FOR GUITAR

Sor/Segovia

20 studies for the classical guitar written by Beethoven's contemporary, Fernando Sor, revised, edited and fingered by the great classical guitarist Andres Segovia. These essential repertoire pieces continue to be used by teachers and students to build solid classical technique. Features a 50-minute demonstration CD.

_____ 00695012 Book/CD Pack $18.95
_____ 00006363 Book Only $7.95

THE FRANCISCO COLLECTION TÁRREGA

edited and performed by Paul Henry

Considered the father of modern classical guitar, Francisco Tárrega revolutionized guitar technique and composed a wealth of music that will be a cornerstone of classical guitar repertoire for centuries to come. This unique book/CD pack features 14 of his most outstanding pieces in standard notation and tab, edited and performed on CD by virtuoso Paul Henry. Includes: Adelita • Capricho Árabe • Estudio Brillante • Grand Jota • Lágrima • Malagueña • María • Recuerdos de la Alhambra • Tango • and more, plus bios of Tárrega and Henry.

_____ 00698993 Book/CD Pack $19.99

HAL • LEONARD® CORPORATION

7777 W. BLUEMOUND RD. P.O. BOX 13819 MILWAUKEE, WI 53213

Visit Hal Leonard Online at **www.halleonard.com**

Prices, contents and availability subject to change without notice.